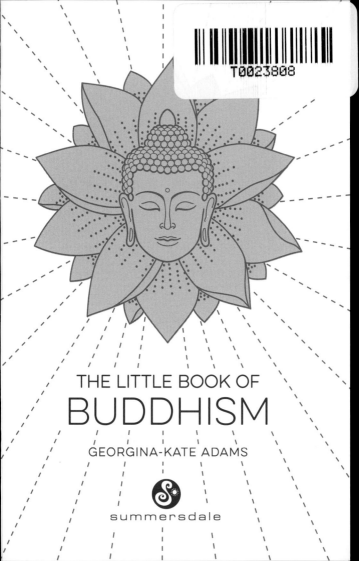

THE LITTLE BOOK OF
BUDDHISM

GEORGINA-KATE ADAMS

summersdale

THE LITTLE BOOK OF BUDDHISM

An Hachette UK Company
www.hachette.co.uk

Summersdale Publishers Ltd
Part of Octopus Publishing Group Limited
Carmelite House
50 Victoria Embankment
LONDON
EC4Y 0DZ
UK

www.summersdale.com

Printed in Malaysia

ISBN: 978-1-80007-707-2

Substantial discounts on bulk quantities of Summersdale books are available to corporations, professional associations and other organizations. For details contact general enquiries: telephone: +44 (0) 1243 771107 or email: enquiries@summersdale.com.

CONTENTS

INTRODUCTION

Buddhism is a religion that many people have heard about without really knowing about it. You may have seen statues of the Buddha for sale in home decor shops – or even have one in your garden – without really knowing what he symbolizes. What is Buddhism? What do Buddhists believe? Who was the Buddha? What are the common practices of Buddhism? And how can I start introducing some basic Buddhist practices into my life? If you have any of these questions, you are in the right place. The answers you seek lie within the pages ahead.

This *Little Book of Buddhism* is, as the name suggests, a "beginner's" guide. It is not a textbook for following Buddhist practices, but rather a starter to whet your appetite and to help you to decide if you would like to pursue further study. Alas, you may not find the secret to realizing "nirvāṇa" in these 128 pages. (Sorry!) What you will find is an introduction to the core beliefs and values of Buddhism, which can help you to live a kinder, happier and more mindful life. Let's dive in!

DO NOT TRY TO
USE WHAT YOU
LEARN FROM
BUDDHISM TO BE
A BUDDHIST. USE
IT TO BE A BETTER
WHATEVER YOU
ALREADY ARE.

THE DALAI LAMA (XIV)

CHAPTER ONE:
WHAT IS BUDDHISM?

Buddhism is the fourth-largest religion on Earth, with about half a billion followers. Originating in ancient India around 2,500 years ago, Buddhism soon spread across Asia. Today, most Buddhists still reside in Asia.

The religion encompasses various beliefs and traditions. All strands of Buddhism, however, are rooted in the teachings of the Buddha, Siddhārtha Gautama (who we will learn about in Chapter Two).

Buddhists believe that nothing in life is perfect and that discontent, illness, ageing and death are fundamental aspects of existence. However, the Buddha taught that the suffering these experiences cause is produced by our own attachments and cravings. For example, most of us are attached to the idea that health is good and sickness bad. Consequently, when we are unwell we may feel upset, wish away our symptoms and crave being healthy again. Yet these emotions may cause us more suffering – by increasing our frustration and discontent.

Buddhists believe that, by overcoming craving and attachment, one can become liberated from suffering – a process known as attaining "enlightenment". This state of freedom from all suffering is called "nirvāṇa".

WHAT DO BUDDHISTS BELIEVE?

Unlike most other major religions, Buddhists do not believe in any kind of god, per se. Rather, Buddhists try to live a good life by following teachings that originated with the Buddha, Siddhārtha Gautama.

Siddhārtha Gautama was an Asian aristocrat who lived in the fifth or sixth century BCE. Horrified by the suffering that he saw in the world, Siddhārtha left his life of luxury to live among holy men and to seek truth. At the age of 35, he became enlightened and he dedicated the rest of his life to spreading the answers he had found. These are contained in what have become known as the "Four Noble Truths" and the "Noble Eightfold Path". (We will learn more about these in Chapter Three.)

Like Hindus and Sikhs, Buddhists believe that we will each have another life (or lives) after this one, but Buddhists see this cycle of rebirth as a negative experience. As such, the majority of Buddhist practices are focused on trying to realize "nirvāṇa", which they believe will end the cycle of rebirth. The techniques used to pursue this include meditation, observing Buddhist ethics and becoming a Buddhist monk or nun.

The Buddha taught that by attaining enlightenment and realizing nirvāṇa, individuals will be able to escape the cycle of rebirth forever. Buddhists believe that life is a constant wheel of suffering and rebirth, and that one is reborn into a different body each time. A human may be reborn as another human or into the body of an animal – or they may be reborn into another spiritual realm entirely.

Kindness and karma

Buddhists believe that how they are reborn will be determined by how they conducted themselves in their previous lives. This relates to "karma": the concept that our past actions affect us, either negatively or positively, and that the actions we take in the present will affect us in the future.

Buddhists believe that kind, generous and mindful actions will help them to develop wholesome karma, which will increase their chance of a favourable rebirth and may even move them a step closer to realizing nirvāṇa. By contrast, unkind, greedy or deluded actions are believed to generate unwholesome karma, which may lead to being born into an unfavourable situation in the next life.

Some people believe that wholesome or unwholesome karma can also lead to positive or negative effects in this life. This provides Buddhists with motivation to be mindful of their actions and to try to live lives of benevolence and compassion.

To guide them in living what they term a "skilful" life and generating wholesome karma, Buddhists follow a code of conduct known as the "Five Precepts". These are vows or promises that Buddhists make when they join the religion. The first precept is to "refrain from killing or harming others" and is one of the reasons why many Buddhists (including most Buddhist monks and nuns) do not eat meat or fish and instead maintain a vegetarian diet.

This first precept is often referred to as "ahiṃsā", its name in Sanskrit (a classical language of South Asia). This translates as "non-violence". Non-violence is a primary virtue of Buddhism, as the pain that violence brings to other living beings may be seen as breaking one's Buddhist vows.

Rather, Buddhists aim to regard all people and animals with compassion. (This is why you may see a Buddhist letting bugs or flies caught in a room out of a window, whereas a non-Buddhist might swot them!) In general, Buddhism is a peaceful tradition that wants happiness and freedom from suffering for all living beings.

HOW PREVALENT IS BUDDHISM?

You may know that Buddhism is popular in regions such as Tibet and Thailand. But did you know that, historically, Buddhism was also widely practised in Afghanistan, the Maldives and Uzbekistan? Indeed, in the modern day, the Buddhist faith has over 520 million followers worldwide – over 7 per cent of the global population. This makes Buddhism the fourth-largest religion in the world.

Today's Buddhist-majority countries are Cambodia (with almost 97 per cent of the nation identifying as Buddhist), Thailand (93 per cent), Myanmar (80 per cent), Bhutan (75 per cent), Sri Lanka (69 per cent), Laos (64 per cent) and Mongolia (55 per cent). Yet due to its enormous population, China has the most followers of Buddhism of any single nation, at nearly 255 million people – making it the home of almost half of all Buddhists on the globe.

Buddhism is also popular in Malaysia, Vietnam, Nepal, Japan and South Korea. Surprisingly, despite being the site of much Buddhist history, modern India has a smaller percentage of Buddhists (0.7 per cent) than the United States (1.2 per cent) – and far fewer than Australia and New Zealand. Almost

3 per cent of the population of Australia identify as Buddhists.

Although Buddhism has an extensive reach across the globe, the countries where the religion is widely practised do not all subscribe to the same traditions and schools of thought. The Theravāda branch of Buddhism is practised most prominently in Sri Lanka, Cambodia, Laos, Myanmar and Thailand, whereas the Mahāyāna branch has the most widespread following in Nepal, Malaysia, Bhutan, China, Japan, South Korea, Vietnam and Mongolia. (We will learn more about these different branches of Buddhism in the following pages.)

In many Western nations, Buddhism has been on the rise since the early twentieth century, when Buddhist societies and temples were first established in Europe. More recently, interest in the religion in the West has been amplified by the popularity of Buddhist figures such as the Dalai Lama (XIV) and the Vietnamese monk and peace activist Thích Nhất Hạnh. Budding Western Buddhists may find that they have to adapt their thinking more than Asian Buddhists, however, as ideas of karma and rebirth are not commonly integrated into Western culture.

WHAT ARE THE DIFFERENT BRANCHES OF BUDDHISM?

Most religions have various branches or "sects" – each having slightly different belief systems or traditions, or placing more or less emphasis on certain teachings. For example, in Christianity the major denominations are Catholic, Protestant, Anglican and Orthodox, while Islam's dominant schools are Sunni and Shi'a. In Buddhism, two major branches have survived to the present: Theravāda and Mahāyāna.

Theravāda Buddhism

Originating in ancient India, Theravāda is Buddhism's oldest existing branch. "Theravāda" is a Pāli word (a classical Indian language and the sacred tongue of Theravāda Buddhism), and roughly translates as "the School of the Elders".

The practices of Theravāda are informed by the earliest Buddhist teachings and adhere closely to the life and lessons of the Buddha, Gautama. Indeed, the holy book of this branch of Buddhism is the Pāli Canon – a compilation of sacred texts that is thought to be the oldest surviving collection of recorded sayings of the Buddha.

The Pāli Canon provides a foundational text for Theravāda Buddhists (known as Theravādins) to follow. Also referred to as the Pāli Tipiṭaka, meaning "the three baskets", this sacred text is divided into three sections:

- The Vinaya Piṭaka: The code for monastic life. These 227 rules are followed by Theravādin monks and nuns, who recite them twice a month.
- The Sutta Piṭaka: The largest basket. It includes accounts of hundreds of oral teachings by the Buddha and his senior disciples, as well as some religious poetry. This basket contains all the fundamental Buddhist philosophies and ethics.
- The Abidhamma Piṭaka: Supplementary philosophies and religious teachings, which are thought to have come later than the first two sections. Theravādin monks place high value on memorizing sections of these texts.

Theravāda teachings and practice

Although the Pāli Canon is regarded as "the word of the Buddha", this is not meant literally, as it also includes the teachings of his senior disciples. Indeed, none of the Canon was written down until approximately 450 years after the Buddha's death. Until then, the teachings were preserved orally by the Buddhist "Sangha" (successive generations of monks and nuns). The Canon was finally written down on palm leaves in Sri Lanka in 29 BCE, and it has since been preserved in text for over two millennia.

The Theravāda approach to Buddhism emphasizes individual enlightenment. In religions such as Christianity or Hinduism, devotees may call on their god (or gods) to aid their self-development. By contrast, Theravādins are taught that they must attain enlightenment through personal effort.

An important part of the Canon is the "Noble Eightfold Path" (which we will learn more about in Chapter Three). This collection of practices provides Buddhists with a structure to follow in their journey toward "arhatship". "Arhat" means "accomplished one" in Pāli.

Arhat is the name given to a person who, like the Buddha, has realized nirvāṇa and freed themselves from the cycle of rebirth. Arhatship relates to the teaching of "anatman" or "no-self". In the Theravādin tradition, this is translated as meaning that an individual's personality or ego is a delusion. It is the cause of their suffering and prevents them from attaining enlightenment.

For Theravādins, time spent in meditation is very important, as this is considered the principal means of shedding the ego and achieving enlightenment. The most common meditation techniques used by Theravādins are "Samatha" and "Vipassanā".

In Samatha, or "mind-calmness" meditation, the meditator tries to focus their mind by concentrating on their breathing. The aim is to deepen focus and to cultivate a temporary feeling of calmness. Vipassanā or "insight" meditation emphasizes disciplined self-observation of the thoughts and emotions, of bodily sensations, and of how these two phenomena interconnect. Vipassanā aims to provide insight into the true nature of reality and to facilitate a complete and permanent change in how the meditator perceives and understands the universe.

Following Theravāda

As well as being Buddhism's oldest branch, Theravāda is also the religion's most conservative arm. Theravādins are loyal to the word of the Buddha, as preserved in the doctrine of the Pāli Canon. They do not accept or practice the teachings of any other prominent Buddhists and reject the authenticity of the Mahāyāna sūtras or scriptures, which appeared from the first century BCE (over 300 years after the Buddha's death).

In Theravāda, however, the scriptures of the Pāli Canon are not seen as having merit on their own, but rather in their application. The teachings captured within it are seen as tools to help people to understand the truth of life.

Theravāda Buddhism is also conservative when it comes to the discipline expected of its monks and nuns, who are required to follow strict rules and procedures. These traditionally include not eating after midday and not handling money. What's more, Theravādins generally believe that only monks and nuns, who have dedicated their life to the study and practice of the scriptures, can attain enlightenment in this lifetime.

An ordinary person studying Theravāda Buddhism, someone who has not given their life to monkhood, is known as a "lay person". Lay people who follow Theravāda are not expected to immediately attain enlightenment. Instead, through their study and practice, they can work toward being reborn in a better state after this life, and perhaps get a step closer to realizing nirvāṇa.

Both monks and lay people play an important role in upholding the Theravādin tradition. Arguably, this tradition couldn't survive without the interaction between them. Lay people support their local monks' focus on their meditation practice by catering for their daily needs: providing them with food, medicine and cloth for their robes. In return, Theravādin monks offer lay people teachings, blessings and spiritual support. Neither party is allowed to request anything from the other. Rather, it is a mutually supportive relationship, based on a spirit of open-hearted giving.

Theravāda ceremonies

The ceremonies of Theravāda Buddhism primarily focus on the life events of the Buddha. These include Wesak (also spelled Vesak), the most sacred and holy day of the calendar for Theravādins. Wesak commemorates the birth, enlightenment and "parinirvāṇa" or passing away of the Buddha. It is observed on the full moon day of the lunar month Vesakha, which falls in May (or sometimes April) each year.

Theravādins celebrate Wesak, also called "Buddha Day", by cleaning and decorating their homes and temples. They converge on temples to listen to teachings and to give food, candles or flowers to monks. Chanting and prayer also feature in the festival.

During Wesak, Buddhists will make an extra effort to donate to charity or help those in need, and vegetarian food is eaten all week. In Indonesia and Thailand, Wesak lanterns are also made, using wood and paper.

Another significant full moon in the Theravādin calendar is the first one in April each year. This turning of the lunisolar calendar is celebrated as the Theravāda New Year, just as other people around the world celebrate 1 January as the start of a new year.

In Sri Lanka, where Theravāda Buddhism is the national religion, every single full moon day is treated as a ceremonial holiday – not only Wesak and Theravāda New Year. Known as Poya Days, each month's full moon has its own name and is linked to a specific event in Buddhist history. These include the anniversaries of the Buddha's enlightenment, when Buddhism first came to Sri Lanka, and of the first Buddhist council, among many other commemorations. In Sri Lanka, every Poya Day is a public holiday and Buddhists dedicate them to their concentrated practice.

Theravāda Buddhism is especially popular in Southeast Asia and, consequently, is sometimes referred to as "Southern Buddhism". As with Sri Lanka, Theravāda is also the official religion in Cambodia, and is the predominant form of Buddhism practised in Laos, Myanmar and Thailand. It is also practised by minorities in India, Nepal, Bangladesh, China and Vietnam – as well as by the diaspora and by converts around the world.

Mahāyāna Buddhism

Mahāyāna is the name for a broad group of Buddhist traditions, philosophies, texts and practices. This collection includes Vajrayāna Buddhism, Zen Buddhism, Tibetan Buddhism and Pure Land Buddhism, among many others. Consequently, Mahāyāna is officially the most popular school of Buddhism existing today. At least 53 per cent of all Buddhists worldwide follow some form of Mahāyāna.

Mahāyāna's origins are not precisely known. Scholars believe that this school emerged in India between the first century BCE and the first century CE, which is when the Mahāyāna sūtras (scriptures) first began to appear.

The Mahāyāna sūtras are believed to have been largely composed in ancient India, although they are predominantly preserved in the Chinese and Tibetan Buddhist canons. Mahāyāna Buddhists (known as Mahāyānists) consider several of the main scriptures as having been taught by the Buddha, Gautama, and memorized by his disciples. Further Mahāyāna sūtras are understood to have been taught by other respected Buddhist teachers.

It is believed that Mahāyāna Buddhism initially existed alongside Theravāda, before eventually becoming a separate tradition. Both Mahāyāna and Theravāda are rooted in the basic teachings of the Buddha and both traditions highlight the individual search for enlightenment. However, the methods they promote for doing this can be very different.

Mahāyāna means "Great Vehicle" in Sanskrit. This name refers to the idea of seeking enlightenment in order to help not just oneself but all sentient beings. These are all beings with consciousness: both humans and animals.

Mahāyāna Buddhists believe that all sentient beings inherently possess "buddha-nature". All possess the "seed" of awakening. Thus, according to the Mahāyāna tradition, any such being (not just a monk or nun) is capable of realizing nirvāṇa within their current lifetime. This sits in contrast with Theravāda, which teaches that enlightenment may only be reached in gradual stages, and that realizing nirvāṇa may take many lifetimes of practice.

The goal of Mahāyāna

Mahāyāna Buddhism is also known as the "Bodhisattva Vehicle". A "bodhisattva" is a being who has attained enlightenment, but postpones being liberated from the cycle of rebirth in order to remain on Earth and teach others how to realize nirvāṇa. The ideal goal of Mahāyāna is for all sentient beings to be enlightened together. This vision is not only inspired by compassion, but by a belief that all life is interconnected.

In Mahāyāna, great emphasis is placed on bodhisattvas as role models. This is a distinct difference with Theravāda, which values only the teachings of the Buddha himself (and his closest disciples). Whereas the Theravādin tradition urges its followers to focus on their own individual awakening, in Mahāyāna followers are encouraged to assist each other to attain enlightenment.

Another distinction is the "roadmap" that each tradition believes provides the best route to enlightenment. Both utilize the teachings of the "Noble Eightfold Path", but according to the Mahāyāna sūtras, to reach the stage of full enlightenment one must follow the "Bodhisattva Path".

MAY ALL BEINGS HAVE HAPPY MINDS.

GAUTAMA BUDDHA

The Bodhisattva Path

At first glance, it may appear that a bodhisattva is the same as an arhat (in Theravāda), as both have attained enlightenment, or, indeed, even the same as a buddha – as the word "buddha" directly translates as "enlightened one". (Hence Siddhārtha Gautama only became known as the Buddha after he had attained enlightenment.) However, in Mahāyāna, there are different levels of awakening.

Mahāyānists certainly revere anyone who has become an arhat, as it is very difficult to reach this stage of spiritual development. Yet in Mahāyāna this is not considered to be the end of the journey. Despite having realized nirvāṇa, an arhat is still considered to have some imperfections. For example, an arhat may still be subject to ignorance, or be capable of being led astray or of relapsing. According to the Mahāyāna tradition, the next step for an arhat is to continue their journey as a bodhisattva. Mahāyānists believe that the only way one can experience full awakening is to follow the Bodhisattva Path.

An intriguing element of the Bodhisattva Path is that anyone can become an "unenlightened bodhisattva" and attempt the journey toward eventually becoming an "enlightened bodhisattva", and finally a full buddha. Yet this journey is not an easy one. On the Bodhisattva Path there are 51 different levels of enlightenment, or stairs to climb. This compares to the process of becoming an arhat in the Theravāda tradition, in which there are only four levels of enlightenment.

The bodhisattva journey begins by taking vows and adopting "the mind of a bodhisattva". This mindset has three key elements: aspiration for awakening; great compassion for all sentient beings; and skilful means. The last of these includes kind words, giving, altruism and empathy, so that all sentient beings may be happy.

Compassion is very important in the Mahāyāna tradition. Indeed, one's motivation for becoming a bodhisattva should be a desire to liberate all beings from the suffering of life, by freeing them from the cycle of rebirth. This is the goal of pursuing the Bodhisattva Path.

Mahāyāna teaching and practice

Perhaps the most important teaching for those on the Bodhisattva Path is that of the "Six Perfections". These are: giving, morality, patience, diligence, meditative concentration and "prajna-wisdom".

Prajna-wisdom is the wherewithal to understand "śūnyatā" (often translated as "emptiness") – a concept at the heart of all Mahāyāna Buddhist teaching. Essentially, it is the same as the Theravādin teaching of anatman or "no-self". However, in Mahāyāna it is translated differently, to suggest that all phenomena – including all humans and animals – are without inherent existence or independent nature. They are more like "illusions". To put it another way: nothing is anything until compared to something else. Realizing śūnyatā is said to be the door to enlightenment.

Whereas Theravādin practice has a strong focus on meditation, the central practice of Mahāyānists is to work on acquiring merit by perfecting the qualities of an "enlightened one". That said, Mahāyānists do practise meditation – this being the fifth of the six perfections. Another key part of their practice is listening to, copying, memorizing, reciting and preaching the Mahāyāna sūtras.

Schools of Mahāyāna

A key distinction between the doctrines of Mahāyāna and Theravāda Buddhism is that, whereas the Pāli Canon is fixed, the Mahāyāna sūtras are dynamic. They have been expanded by different cultures and in some cases even blended with Indigenous folk religions. Hence, when reviewing the various Mahāyāna schools, there is a broad array of teachings and activities to be found.

When we talk about Mahāyāna Buddhism, we talk about an umbrella under which many hundreds of different schools of Buddhism fall. Each of these schools hold their own ideas, traditions and forms of practice (albeit with overlaps between them). What they have in common is that they all accept the Mahāyāna sūtras. They all also broadly share the philosophy that the route to enlightenment is to follow the Bodhisattva Path. In addition, unlike Theravādins, followers of Mahāyāna schools generally believe that there are many buddhas and that these exist in a spiritual realm beyond the physical world.

You may be wondering: what are all these different schools of Mahāyāna? Let's review some of the most popular. In doing so, it is important to note that within these traditions, there are often smaller schools as well.

Zen Buddhism

A combination of Mahāyāna Buddhism and Taoism, Zen Buddhism emerged in China in the fifth century CE. It soon spread to Korea and Japan, and more recently has become very popular in Western nations.

Zen Buddhists believe that the truth needed to attain enlightenment cannot be found in rational thought, scriptures or religious rituals, but that all the answers we need are within ourselves.

Zen teachers often assign their students "koans". Koans are seemingly nonsensical words or phrases – such as "show me your face before your parents were born" – which when used as an object for meditation are said to help one to awaken.

It has been said that Zen cannot be explained in words and must be experienced to be understood. This tradition has a strong focus on meditation, with the goal of freeing the mind of words and logical thinking and allowing one's inner buddha to emerge.

Vajrayāna Buddhism

Vajrayāna is a tradition based on mysterious Indian texts called "tantras", which are designed to offer a rapid route to enlightenment. This school is thought to have originated in India in the fifth century CE – although some Buddhists believe that it was taught by the Buddha himself.

Often referred to as the "Diamond Vehicle" or "Indestructible Vehicle", Vajrayāna is also known as "Tantric Buddhism" or "Secret Mantra". The Vajrayāna teachings are kept a closely guarded secret, as they are said to be so powerful that they could be dangerous if applied wrongly. Only skilled meditators may be taught them and this must be done directly by an experienced "lama" (teacher).

Buddhists who join this school are expected to exhibit intense dedication to their practice. Common Vajrayāna practices utilize mantras, mandalas, visualization and chanting.

This tradition is particularly popular in the Himalayan region – especially Tibet and Nepal – as well as in Mongolia and in other parts of East Asia.

Tibetan Buddhism

Originating in the seventh century CE, Tibetan Buddhism remains the dominant religion in Tibet and Bhutan. It also has many followers in other regions surrounding the Himalayas, as well as in Central Asia, southern Siberia and Mongolia.

Tibetan Buddhism is often misunderstood as being identical to Vajrayāna, but this is not correct. Rather, Tibetan Buddhism combines elements of Vajrayāna with Shamanism, an ancient Tibetan religion called Bon, and the essential teachings of Mahāyāna. This combination of belief systems perhaps explains the strong presence of supernatural beings within this tradition.

A popular Tibetan Buddhist practice involves meditating on a chosen deity, including reciting mantras and prayers. Rituals are also important to Tibetan Buddhists. These often involve visual aids, such as prayer flags or prayer wheels, which offer a physical, ever-present reminder of the spiritual world in daily life.

The figurehead of this tradition is the Dalai Lama (XIV), who is the spiritual leader of the Gelug school.

Pure Land Buddhism

Starting in India in the second century BCE, Pure Land Buddhism is especially popular in China, Japan and Korea. Its main practice is chanting the name of "Amitābha Buddha" with concentration, sincerity and complete faith, in the belief that this will lead to being reborn in the "Pure Land".

Amitābha Buddha is an enlightened being whose name means "Immeasurable Light", and who is regarded by Pure Land Buddhists as a kind of saviour. He is the buddha of comprehensive love and infinite life.

The Pure Land is said to be a spiritual domain generated by Amitābha Buddha, where one can study directly with him and, consequently, swiftly reach enlightenment. The Pure Land should not be confused with a paradise, like the Christian idea of heaven. It is not the desired final destination of followers. The Pure Land is, instead, a place that is believed to be just a step away from realizing nirvāṇa.

Mahāyāna ceremonies

Like Theravādins, Mahāyānists also celebrate the Buddha's birthday. But unlike Wesak, Mahāyānists mark the birth, enlightenment and passing away of the Buddha separately. During the Buddha's birthday celebration, Mahāyānists perform a ritual called "Bathing the Buddha". Scented water is poured over the shoulders of a statue of the Buddha as a baby. This is a symbolic reminder for Buddhists to purify their own minds of ignorance, hatred and greed.

Another important date in the Mahāyāna calendar is Parinirvāṇa Day, which marks the anniversary of the Buddha's physical death, at age 80. Celebrated in February, this is the day that the Buddha entered the final stage of nirvāṇa (parinirvāṇa) and escaped the cycle of rebirth forever. You may have seen images or statues of the Buddha lying down, and these depict his parinirvāṇa. During this celebration, Mahāyānists visit temples and monasteries and take gifts to the monks and nuns. Passages from the "nirvāṇa sūtra" are recited, people reflect on death, and meditation is practised.

The Buddha's enlightenment is celebrated by Mahāyānists in December or January (depending on the lunar calendar). Known as Bodhi Day, Mahāyānists spend this celebration focusing hard on their meditation, chanting and reciting the scriptures. Lay people may also eat special meals at this time.

Mahāyāna New Year is also celebrated in January, although (as is true with the Theravāda New Year) the exact date varies by country. Some Mahāyānists observe the Gregorian New Year on 1 January, while others wait for January's full moon.

These important dates are marked differently according to location, and according to the specific school of Mahāyāna Buddhism predominantly practised there. Asia's main contemporary Mahāyāna traditions can be broadly split into two groups: "Eastern Buddhism" and "Northern Buddhism".

Eastern Buddhism, the largest group, encapsulates the East Asian Mahāyāna traditions of China, Japan, Korea and Vietnam. Northern Buddhism refers to the Indo-Tibetan traditions found in Tibet, Bhutan and Mongolia, and in parts of Nepal and India. Yet more schools exist outside of these classifications. Mahāyāna is also practised by Asian Buddhists in the diaspora, as well as by Western converts.

As this chapter has shown, there is no "one way" to practise Buddhism. It depends on the needs of the individual. Indeed, it is the religion's very capacity for adaptation that has allowed for its adoption by so many different cultures – and its continued relevance to the present day.

Crucially, the different Buddhist schools generally practise tolerance for each others' beliefs and activities, in the knowledge that they have a shared aim. Imagine that you had lost your cat and went door-knocking on your street to see if anyone had found it. If your sibling knocked on a different door to you, you wouldn't resent them for it. You would wish them luck! You are looking for the same thing, after all. Similarly, Buddhists are united around a common goal of finding freedom. It is understood that there may be many doors to realizing nirvāṇa and, essentially, that the various Buddhist schools are knocking on different ones.

Ultimately, all Buddhists – whether Theravādins or Mahāyānists – are guided by the Four Noble Truths and the Noble Eightfold Path. They attend each others' events and can even be found worshipping peacefully together in the same temples.

SEEK PEACE.
WHEN YOU HAVE
PEACE WITHIN,
REAL PEACE
WITH OTHERS
IS POSSIBLE.

THÍCH NHẤT HẠNH

CHAPTER TWO:
A BRIEF HISTORY
OF BUDDHISM

Having learned about the main beliefs and branches of Buddhism, you may want to discover more about this mysterious man that we know as the Buddha. In this chapter, we will do just that! His is a tale so captivating that it has been turned into works of fiction, audiobooks and bedtime stories.

One of the most compelling aspects of the Buddha's story is that, unlike other key religious leaders, Siddhārtha Gautama was not chosen or sent by a god to fulfil their will on Earth. Although some intriguing myths surround him, Siddhārtha was ultimately just a man who couldn't bear to see the suffering in the world and wanted to find a solution. Thus his is a path that is accessible to all of us.

What is also remarkable is how this one man's spiritual journey attracted so many millions of followers around the world and birthed a religion that has continued for over 2,500 years after his death – and counting! In this chapter, we will discover how his teachings attracted such a huge following, and how this led to the development of the various Buddhist schools of thought.

THE STORY OF THE BUDDHA

The tale of the Buddha's life is an enchanting one and has inspired millions of people around the globe. It is informed by early Buddhist texts, yet it is important to note that these accounts are inconsistent, difficult to prove and prone to debate. Thus his story must be taken with a pinch of salt – and a willingness to allow some mystery to remain.

What we can reasonably speculate is that the man that we know today as the Buddha was born in Kapilavastu City in the fifth or sixth century BCE. Kapilavastu is found in Lumbini, which is a region of modern-day Nepal.

The Buddha was born with the status of a prince and named Siddhārtha Gautama. His father, Śuddhodana, was the elected leader of the Shakya clan. His mother Māyā was the princess of a different clan and is praised in Buddhist texts for her beauty.

Legend has it that, for 20 years, Māyā and Śuddhodana had no children. Then, one night, Māyā dreamed about a white elephant with six white tusks that entered her right side. She took this as a good omen and, indeed, ten months later,

Siddhārtha was born. The baby arrived underneath a Sal tree, in a garden in Lumbini.

Holy men quickly predicted that the child was destined for greatness – either as a profound religious figure or ruler. His birth name, "Siddhārtha", echoes this prophecy. Formed of two Sanskrit words, "siddha" means "achieved" and "artha" means "what was searched for". The complete name translates as "he who has attained his goals" or "he who has found meaning (of existence)".

Just a week after Siddhārtha's birth, his mother died. Māyā's younger sister, Mahāprajāpatī (Siddhārtha's aunt), became Śuddhodana's wife and she raised Siddhārtha as if he were her own child.

Growing up, Siddhārtha enjoyed a luxurious life, with the best diet and a different home for each season. He was spoiled, as he told his monks years later.

The adolescent Siddhārtha was apparently an intelligent young man, a skilled athlete and martial artist. At the age of 16, he got married to his cousin, Yaśodhrā.

The Four Sights

Siddhārtha's life was one of luxury, but it was also sheltered, for his father forbid him from leaving his family's estate. Of the predictions about Siddhārtha's future, Śuddhodana hoped that his son would follow in his footsteps and become a great ruler. Yet he feared that, should Siddhārtha be exposed to the suffering of the outside world, he may be inspired to become a holy man instead. To avoid this, Śuddhodana kept his son locked away in a life of privilege and perfection. He also tried to keep religious teachings from him.

For nearly 30 years, Śuddhodana's plan worked, until, at the age of 29, Siddhārtha grew disillusioned with his luxurious life, finding it empty, and became curious about the world beyond the gates of the estate.

One day, Siddhārtha persuaded his chariot driver, whose name was Channa, to take him into the city. There he had what are now known as the "Four Sights": his introduction to the notion of suffering.

In the city, Siddhārtha saw an elderly person for the first time in his life. He was horrified, for he knew nothing of ageing. He asked Channa what he was seeing and the driver explained that as people grow older their bodies decline.

Siddhārtha asked to be taken home. Yet before long, curiosity led the young man to venture out into the city again. This time he saw a diseased person at the side of the road. Siddhārtha was deeply distressed, for he knew nothing of illness either. During their lives people get ill, Channa explained.

On his next trip, Siddhārtha saw a dead person, being carried as part of a funeral procession. Once more, Channa explained that everybody will die eventually. Then, Siddhārtha saw an "ascetic" (a holy man who lives a life of self-denial and truth-seeking).

Siddhārtha observed the ascetic with interest. He was moved by how calm and serene the man appeared, despite the chaos and suffering in the streets around them. This experience was the start of Siddhārtha's own spiritual journey.

Siddhārtha's spiritual journey

The Four Sights became the catalyst for Siddhārtha to make a bold move. One night, without telling anyone, he and Channa left the estate on horseback – thus abandoning his privileged life and loving family in order to live as a wandering ascetic and search for answers. Siddhārtha even left behind his baby son, Rāhula, who had been born the very same evening, leaving his wife, Yaśodhrā, devastated.

Together, Siddhārtha and Channa travelled to the Anoma River. Once across, Siddhārtha cut off his hair and abandoned his princely dress for the robes of an ascetic. Then he left Channa and his horse behind and journeyed into the woods to begin his new existence as a monk.

Siddhārtha's day-to-day life was now very different. For some years he allegedly lived in remote jungle thickets – which could be frightening places. He also had to beg for "alms", donations of food and other items from lay people, who, as part of their own spiritual practice, give to monks as an act of virtue.

Siddhārtha sought spiritual teachers and was taught yogic meditation by the hermit Āḷāra Kāmāla. Soon he was equal in skill to his master and had nothing more to learn from him. Āḷāra asked Siddhārtha to become co-leader of his spiritual community and to teach his students, but Siddhārtha refused. He had become dissatisfied with the practice, because it did not lead to awakening. Thus he continued with his quest.

His next teacher was the sage Uddaka Rāmaputta, another teacher of yogic meditation. Uddaka quickly identified Siddhārtha as not his student but his superior. He asked him to become the sole leader of his community, but Siddhārtha had still not found what he was looking for and moved on.

Siddhārtha then began a period of severe asceticism. Asceticism is a form of extreme self-discipline, which includes avoiding any forms of indulgence or sensual pleasure, for the purpose of achieving a spiritual goal. For Siddhārtha, this included forceful breath and mind control, and long periods of fasting. He wanted to understand the nature of suffering.

The turning point

Siddhārtha took his frugal approach to such an extreme that his once-strong body was soon reduced to skin and bone. He realized then that starvation had neither helped him to realize nirvāṇa, nor given him the strength he needed to pursue his goal. This experience would later lead the Buddha to promote a spiritual path known as the "Middle Way": a life of moderation rather than of total scarcity and poverty.

Once he had regained his strength, Siddhārtha, feeling closer to his goal, sat down beneath a fig tree with the determination not to get up until he had reached full awakening. For a week he sat beneath that tree (now known as the "Bodhi tree") and it was here that he realized nirvāṇa and became the Buddha: an enlightened being or "one who is awake". He was 35 years old.

After his enlightenment, the Buddha was unsure whether he should attempt to teach what he had learned to others. He felt that most humans were so overpowered by ignorance, greed and hatred that they could not appreciate such a subtle path. Yet an encounter with the deity Brahmā Sahampati convinced him to try.

The Buddha's first sermon was to a group of five ascetics, in a deer park near Vārānasī, which is in modern-day India. The content of this sermon was what is now known as the Four Noble Truths. Legend has it that, after hearing this teaching, one of the ascetics himself realized nirvāṇa and became an arhat.

Next, the Buddha taught the holy men about anatman ("no-self"), after which they all became enlightened as arhats too. Consequently, all five of these ascetics decided to become Buddhist monks, forming the first "Sangha" – the name for the Buddhist community.

From here, the Buddha's following continued to grow. By the end of that rainy season, the Sangha had reputedly grown to around 60 monks, all of whom had reached arhat status. When the rains stopped, the Buddha instructed these monks to disperse and disseminate the teachings, to help as many people as possible to achieve freedom from suffering.

Sharing the "Dharma"

For the remaining 45 years of his life, the Buddha travelled across northern India and southern Nepal teaching everyone from kings to servants, from holy men to householders, and even – allegedly – murderers and cannibals. Uniquely, the Buddha made his teachings accessible to everyone, regardless of gender, caste or social status. His teachings became known as the "Dharma", meaning "truth". As he travelled and taught, so the Sangha grew.

The Buddha returned to Kapilavastu, where his own family were touched by his Dharma. His father, Śuddhodana, was so moved by his teachings that he converted to Buddhism. Meanwhile, the Buddha's son, Rāhula, became a Buddhist monk – as did several other members of his family.

Most notably, the Buddha's stepmother, Mahāprajāpatī, became the first woman to seek ordination as a Buddhist nun. This was revolutionary in a time when women had few rights and were seen as inferior to men, although the Buddha himself rejected such inequality. Nonetheless, he at first denied his stepmother's request, fearing that it wasn't safe for women to be wandering ascetics.

It is said that Mahāprajāpatī shaved her head, donned robes and followed the Buddha anyway, until eventually he ordained her as a nun. In doing so, he became the first religious leader to accept female disciples. Mahāprajāpatī went on to attain enlightenment and become an arhat.

Despite declining health, the Buddha continued to teach and develop the Sangha until his final days on Earth. At the age of 80, while travelling with his disciples, the Buddha became so weak that he had to stop in the town of Kushinagar, which is in modern-day India. He lay down in a grove of Sal trees, entered into meditation and passed into parinirvāṇa – the final nirvāṇa, achieved upon death. With this, the Buddha was freed from the cycle of rebirth and suffering forever.

THE DEVELOPMENT OF BUDDHISM

Three months after the Buddha's passing, 500 of his senior monks gathered in Rajgir, in modern-day India, and held what is now referred to as the "First Buddhist Council". The meeting lasted for seven months. During this gathering, members of the council recited, collected and memorized the Buddha's teachings, so as to preserve them. At this first council, the monks also voted to maintain the Vinaya (the code of conduct for monastic life), despite the Buddha having given permission for them to abolish the minor rules.

This first council meeting laid the foundations for what would one day develop into the global religion that we now know as Buddhism. It should not be assumed, however, that Buddhism was established overnight. For over 100 years it remained a minority movement, preserved and practised by the Sangha.

About 70 years after the first meeting, a second Buddhist Council was held to address a set of ten monastic rules that had come under debate. It is alleged that, at this stage, the Sangha began to split into two schools: those who wished to uphold the original Vinaya and those who wished to relax some of the rules.

Over the following few centuries, these divisions continued, with the Sangha establishing about 20 distinct schools of Buddhism. These reflected differing interpretations of the Vinaya and the teachings, and sometimes simply the geographic locations of the monks. Of these early schools, Theravāda is believed to be the only one that has survived to the present day. Mahāyāna Buddhism, meanwhile, is said to have emerged from a combination of some of these early schools and later ones.

It was not until the rule of King Ashoka that Buddhism began to become more established and widespread as a religion. King Ashoka (often referred to as "Ashoka the Great") was an Indian emperor who ruled over almost the entire Indian subcontinent from about 268 to 232 BCE. His Mauryan Empire included modern-day Pakistan, Nepal, the majority of India, and parts of Bangladesh, Afghanistan and Iran.

The Buddhist king

Legend has it that, after years of brutal conquests, a particularly bloody war between the Mauryan Empire and the state of Kalinga proved a turning point for King Ashoka. Upon hearing of the bloodshed – about 250,000 lives were said to have been lost in the battle, including 100,000 of his own warriors – Ashoka is said to have become deeply remorseful and pledged never to wage war again. He converted to Buddhism and became the first Buddhist king.

This change of heart from cruel king to benevolent Buddhist appears noble, although some historians have suggested that Ashoka's adoption of Buddhism may have been a political decision. He needed to unite the diverse array of people, cultures and worldviews within his extensive empire, and Buddhism is a religion that (as we have seen) has the ability to peacefully amalgamate different ideas and values. Whatever his intentions, as an emperor of great power and influence, and with extensive territory under his control, King Ashoka was well-positioned to promote the spread of Buddhism – and he did.

Ashoka used the Buddha's teachings to reform his government and announced a new approach of "conquest by righteousness" (Dharma), rather than by war. New laws were established in line with Ashoka's understanding of Buddhism. These focused on the principles of non-violence, generosity, tolerance of all opinions, respect for elders and spiritual teachers, and more. The kingdom's foreign policy was changed from one of military aggression to one of political discourse and negotiation.

Domestically, the new laws included criminalizing the hunting or wounding of animals, the promotion of vegetarianism, a reduction in corporal punishment, and amnesty for prisoners who were awaiting execution. Ashoka's government also built new hospitals – both for people and animals – as well as constructing universities, free hostels for pilgrims, many new roads, wells and irrigation systems, and public gardens of medicinal herbs.

Ashoka's policies aimed to reduce the suffering of his subjects. Furthermore, following the Buddha's example, the new legislation did not discriminate against anyone due to caste, religion or political alignment.

King Ashoka's influence on Buddhism

The principle priority of King Ashoka's rule became to spread Buddhism, believing that this could help to relieve his subjects of their suffering. Ashoka personally travelled to rural areas to share the Buddha's teachings and he ordered his ministers, administrators and even his sons to do the same.

After his passing, the Buddha's body had been cremated and his ashes and bones distributed between several north Indian kingdoms, where they were kept as sacred relics in commemorative burial mounds or monuments called stupas. After hundreds of years, these remains were unearthed under Ashoka's rule and were enshrined into new stupas that he had constructed throughout his empire. According to early texts, small portions of the seven relics that Ashoka acquired were divided into 84,000 boxes made of fine materials such as gold, silver, crystal and cat's eye. These enabled the creation of 84,000 new holy sites where converts to Buddhism could visit and worship.

King Ashoka also established monuments marking some of the significant sites from the life of the Buddha (such as the location of his first sermon) and constructed many Buddhist monasteries.

At dozens of these holy sites, he erected what are now referred to as the "Pillars of Ashoka" – columns inscribed with proclamations, based on his understanding of the Buddhist teachings. These edicts became the official laws of the empire and would later become a symbol of early Buddhist teachings.

It was King Ashoka who convened the third Buddhist Council in his capital city, Paliputra, although there are contrasting accounts of the nature of this meeting. According to records from the Sarvāstivāda tradition of Buddhism, it was only at this meeting that the first division in the religion occurred. However, according to Theravāda accounts of the event, Ashoka's very motivation for organizing this council was to clean up the many divisions that had already developed within the Buddhist movement. In particular, he was said to be concerned about the emergence of what he saw as corrupt, opportunistic monks and misbelievers, and he wished to remove such people from the Sangha.

Early Buddhist missionaries

During the third council, the key components of the Buddhist doctrine are said to have been decided and formalized. As soon as what was felt to be the true Dharma had been established, King Ashoka launched a grand-scale missionary effort to spread the Buddha's teachings far and wide.

Skilled monks and nuns, who could recite the Dharma by heart, were encouraged to become ambassadors for the religion and to offer the teachings to other lands. Missionaries were sent throughout the Mauryan Empire and beyond. They spread Buddhism into present-day Myanmar, throughout Southeast Asia and China, and even into North Africa and Europe, travelling as far as Greece and Egypt. Ashoka's oldest son, Mahinda, is personally credited for bringing Buddhism to Sri Lanka. Such was Mahinda's dedication to the religion that he later refused to succeed his father on the throne, as he wished to dedicate his life to monkhood.

Under the rule of King Ashoka, Buddhism was elevated from being a minority philosophical movement to, in essence, a state religion. The emperor's loyal patronage for Buddhism allowed the faith to flourish and accelerated its reach both throughout and beyond modern-day India – spreading the Buddha's teachings out into the world.

Although after Ashoka's death and the subsequent collapse of the Mauryan Empire, the popularity of Buddhism significantly declined in India, the global foundations that Ashoka had laid could not be undone. The actions of King Ashoka during the third century BCE played a pivotal role in Buddhism becoming the major world religion that it is today.

Following the era of Ashoka, Buddhism continued to grow in popularity outside of India. Hence it was in Sri Lanka that what Theravādins consider to be the fourth Buddhist Council was held, in the first century BCE. This meeting was reportedly a response to a year of poor harvests in Sri Lanka, following which many Buddhist monks had died of starvation. This led the surviving monks to fear that the oral literature of the Pāli Canon could be lost in the future, if those monks responsible for remembering and transmitting it died before they could pass it on.

Preserving the Dharma

To ensure that the Dharma survived for future generations, the Palī Canon was finally committed to paper during the fourth Buddhist Council in Sri Lanka – or, more specifically, to palm leaves.

About 100 years later, in 78 CE, another council was allegedly held in Kashmir (then a part of the Kushan Empire). According to the Sarvāstivāda tradition of Buddhism, this meeting was the fourth Buddhist Council. In either case, the meeting had a similar purpose to the Sri Lankan council: to systemize and preserve the Dharma.

The Kushan emperor, Kanishka, reportedly assembled 500 male Buddhist monks (or "bhikkhus") to organize and translate the Abhidhamma texts, used by Sarvāstivāda, from earlier vernacular languages into Sanskrit. This process apparently took 12 years to complete and involved compiling millions of statements and verses.

Although the Sarvāstivāda tradition of Buddhism is now extinct, it remains an important piece of Buddhist history, as many of its traditions were ultimately inherited by the Mahāyāna branch. This affected Buddhism's development into the religion we know today.

IF ANYTHING IS WORTH DOING, DO IT WITH ALL YOUR HEART.

GAUTAMA BUDDHA

BUDDHISM AROUND THE WORLD

We have learned that King Ashoka planted the seed of Buddhism around Asia. But how did it grow from there? How did the religion spread to the rest of the world? And how did this expansion influence Buddhism's division into so many new branches of the religion?

By the time of the fourth Buddhist Council, in the first century BCE, it is believed that Buddhism had already split into many schools. As the thoughts and philosophies of the various cultural groups practising Buddhism became more diverse, different branches of the religion were developed. The Dharma became blended with the traditions and cosmologies of the new cultures it encountered and naturally adapted into variations more relevant to those cultures.

This process of expansion, adaptation and amalgamation continued for thousands of years – gradually forming the hundreds of schools of Buddhism present today. So, let's explore how the religion spread throughout Asia, as well as how it reached the West.

Buddhism in East Asia

Although King Ashoka is reported to have spread Buddhism into China, according to Chinese records the religion's formal arrival into the region came around 400 years later, in the first or second century CE. By then, much of modern-day northern India, Pakistan and Afghanistan had become territories of the Kushan Empire, which was a great patron of Buddhism. It is understood that the influence of Kushan missionaries in China led to the Chinese emperor Huan of Han adopting Buddhism as the official religion of the court.

The Buddhism practised in China hence became known as "Han Buddhism" or "Chinese Buddhism": a version that has been influenced by Chinese culture and philosophy – or, more specifically, by Han culture and philosophy (the largest ethnic group in China). All East Asian schools of Buddhism are believed to derive from this branch.

Some of the more influential schools in East Asia include Pure Land, Zen, Tiantai, Huayan and Chinese Esoteric Buddhism. They have in common their focus on the Mahāyāna scriptures and their fresh, distinctly East Asian interpretations of the Dharma.

Buddhism in and around Central Asia

In the mid-second century CE, the Kushan Empire expanded into Central Asia, and Buddhist missionaries quickly began sharing the Dharma in the region. The spread of Buddhism in this area was further influenced by the hive of activity along the Silk Road trade route in the early part of the first millennium CE. This facilitated the exchange of not only goods but of cultures and philosophies, between South, East and Central Asia, and beyond. Much of the transmission of Buddhism along this route is credited to Buddhist monks from Iran, who are also said to have played a significant role in the religion's spread in China during this era.

Earlier still, however, Buddhism was already developing a presence in the region that we now know as Afghanistan, where it was introduced during King Ashoka's rule. Indeed, for centuries, the heart of Central Asian Buddhism was Nava Vihara, a Buddhist monastery in Balkh, Afghanistan. It was only after the nation's conquest by Arab Muslims in the seventh century CE that Buddhism began to decline in Afghanistan, although it took over 600 years for it to be completely eradicated.

Buddhism in Southeast Asia

The earliest accounts of Buddhism in Southeast Asia record King Ashoka's missionaries operating in present-day Myanmar. The mission was embraced by the Mon Kingdom – which encompassed much of modern-day Myanmar, Thailand and the Malaysian Peninsula – and the kingdom became a centre for Theravāda Buddhism.

The Silk Road also greatly helped the spread of Buddhism through mainland Southeast Asia and into its island nations. To this day, those Southeast Asian countries that received Buddhism from the north generally practise Mahāyāna Buddhism, as it was origin schools of Mahāyāna that were prominent in the regions north of them at the time (Central and Eastern Asia, and northern India). For example, Vietnam and the island nations of Southeast Asia predominantly follow Mahāyāna Buddhism.

By contrast, those nations that received Buddhism from the south, such as via trade with southern India and Sri Lanka, mostly practise Theravāda Buddhism. These include Cambodia, Thailand and Laos. That Theravāda also filtered down to these countries from Myanmar illustrates that the lines of influence are not clear-cut, as trade routes ran in all directions.

Buddhism in the West

As a consequence of King Ashoka's missionaries travelling into Greece, the first known Westerners to convert to Buddhism were ancient Greeks. In particular, they were Greeks who had resettled in Central Asia and northern India – an area that later became an ancient Greek kingdom (known historically as Yavana) from 200 BCE to 10 CE. Yavana Kingdom became a patron of Buddhism, leading to the emergence of Greco-Buddhism – a blend of Hellenistic culture and Buddhist belief.

Following the fall of the Yavana Kingdom, there was little contact between the West and Buddhist cultures for around 1,000 years. However, the rise of global trade, as well as the colonization of Asian Buddhist countries by European nations from the eighteenth century CE, led to increased awareness of Buddhism among Westerners. As part of the colonial agenda, attempts were made to force Asian Buddhists to convert to Christianity. Yet Western interest in Buddhism began to rise, and this continued throughout the twentieth century, influenced by increased globalization and immigration. Today, there are many Buddhist converts in the West, although it remains a minority religion there.

SHARE YOUR KNOWLEDGE. IT IS A WAY TO ACHIEVE IMMORTALITY.

THE DALAI LAMA (XIV)

CHAPTER THREE:
THE BUDDHIST
WORLDVIEW

So far in this book we have touched upon many Buddhist teachings and ideas: the concepts of karma, rebirth, nirvāṇa and enlightenment; the Four Noble Truths; and the Noble Eightfold Path, to name but a few. You may now be wondering, for example, what are the Four Noble Truths? Or, what is the difference between enlightenment and awakening?

In this chapter we will dive deeper into some of these ideas, and explore what they are and why they are so important to Buddhists' practice... almost like a one-stop-shop glossary for the trickiest Buddhist terms!

Of course, with so many different traditions of Buddhism comes a wide variety of schools of thought. We cannot cover them all in this chapter. Instead, we will take a brief look at some of the core beliefs, values and practices of Buddhism.

Hopefully, by the end of it, you'll be ready to pass a Buddhism pop quiz![1] Let's do it!

---

[1] Don't worry, there's not really a quiz!

THE FOUR NOBLE TRUTHS

At the heart of all the Buddha's teachings are the Four Noble Truths. These are fundamental truths that the Buddha realized on the night of his enlightenment and were the first lesson that he taught, in his first sermon.

The Four Noble Truths are appreciated by all schools of Buddhism. Buddhists best know them by the Pāli terms "dukkha", "samudāya", "nirodha" and "magga". Let us explore the Four Noble Truths one by one.

Dukkha

Commonly translated as "suffering" or the truth that in life "there is suffering", dukkha more directly translates as "incapable of satisfying". This constant feeling of "unsatisfactoriness" was considered by the Buddha to be the ailment of humans' lives: this is the first noble truth.

Dukkha is not regarded as a suffering experienced occasionally, but as an intrinsic challenge of being human – experienced to a lesser or greater extent in the course of every day.

Samudāya

The second noble truth is that there is a cause for dukkha. According to the Buddha, the root of this feeling of "unsatisfactoriness" is attachment – sometimes also described as "craving" or "thirst".

There are two parts to this. On the one hand, humans crave (and even expect) happiness from states that are impermanent. When pleasant sensations arise, they become attached to them – yet these sensations do not last. Thus, according to the Buddha, because the things that make humans happy go away or change, they can never attain real and lasting happiness.

On the other hand, humans crave avoiding experiences that bring up painful or unpleasant feelings. They may become attached to the idea that things like pain or ill health are bad, not understanding that these too are temporary states. According to the noble truths, both pleasant and unpleasant sensations are changing phenomena, and dukkha arises when humans crave or cling to any one of them.

Nirodha

The third noble truth is that there is an end to suffering. Humans can escape the bind of dukkha by giving up the patterns of craving and attachment that ultimately cause them pain or dissatisfaction. This is seen as one of the fundamental steps – if not the most fundamental step – to realizing nirvāṇa.

This is because dukkha is only experienced by those who are trapped in saṃsāra. (We will learn more about this concept on page 78, but in short, saṃsāra is the constant cycle of rebirth.)

Indeed, according to the noble truths, it is the attachments and cravings of human beings that keep them caught in saṃsāra and the unrelenting dukkha that accompanies it. This cycle also perpetuates the ego-mind: that is, the image we have of ourselves and our habitual tendency to defend it – the idea of a "self" which is separate from others.

The noble truth of nirodha asserts that, upon realizing nirvāṇa, craving will cease, and rebirth and its accompanying dukkha will not arise again. In doing so, a person's true, natural state is said to be revealed.

Magga

The fourth and final noble truth proposes a roadmap that humans can use to navigate their way out of their cycles of craving, dukkha and, ultimately, saṃsāra. The noble truth of magga states that the way to end craving and attachment, and to become free from dukkha, is to follow the Noble Eightfold Path.

The Buddha said that through following the Noble Eightfold Path, humans can learn to limit their automatic responses to sensory contacts – whether pleasant or unpleasant sensations – and learn restraint. According to the Buddha, by cultivating self-discipline, and practising mindfulness and meditation, humans can develop the ability to stop reacting to their cravings and, in doing so, experience freedom from dukkha – ultimately realizing nirvāṇa.

The Four Noble Truths provide a conceptual framework for Buddhist thought. Most Buddhists, however, would not consider these teachings alone to be sufficient for realizing nirvāṇa. Rather, they introduce the basic orientation of Buddhism. For an individual to truly understand the Four Noble Truths, it is believed that they must experience them for themselves.

THE NOBLE EIGHTFOLD PATH

The fourth noble truth tells us that there is a path ("magga") that can be taken to escape human suffering and the cycle of rebirth. According to the Theravāda tradition of Buddhism, the Noble Eightfold Path is the path to liberation: it is the path to becoming enlightened and to becoming an arhat. The Noble Eightfold Path is also important in the Mahāyāna tradition. For Mahāyānists it is explored alongside the Bodhisattva Path.

Almost everything that the Buddha taught came from the Noble Eightfold Path. Although he gave many thousands of sermons during his lifetime, the essence of these are captured in this one text. As such, it can be regarded as an essential summary of his key teachings.

The eight factors that form the Noble Eightfold Path are:

❀ Right View
❀ Right Intention
❀ Right Speech
❀ Right Action

- Right Livelihood
- Right Effort
- Right Mindfulness
- Right Concentration

Despite being presented in the order above, the eight categories of the path are not designed to be followed one by one. Instead, Buddhists work to develop these skills simultaneously, as each factor is linked and helps to support the cultivation of the others. Indeed, the eight elements of the Noble Eightfold Path are often presented in a circle, as the eight spokes of a chariot wheel. This image, known as the "Dharma Wheel," is one of the oldest symbols in Buddhism and has come to represent the religion, in the same way that a Star of David represents Judaism, or a cross represents Christianity.

The eight parts of the Noble Eightfold Path can be further broken down into three categories. Known as the Threefold Way, these are the three essentials of Buddhist discipline, which the Buddha taught constitute the path to enlightenment. They are: ethical conduct (sīla), mental discipline or meditation (samādhi), and wisdom (paññā). It can be easier to understand the Noble Eightfold Path by exploring them under these three divisions.

Ethical conduct (sīla)

- Right Speech: Speaking truthfully, kindly and with careful intention – or else staying silent. Avoiding telling lies, indulging in idle babble or gossip, using rude or abusive language, or talking in a way that could bring about division or hatred.

- Right Action: Acting in a loving, moral and peaceful way – and helping others to do the same. Showing restraint in seeking pleasures and not engaging in dishonest dealings, illegitimate sexual activity or misconduct, theft or the taking of life.

- Right Livelihood: Making a living in a way that does not bring harm to or exploit other living creatures. Not selling harmful items, including lethal weapons or intoxicating drinks, but rather living by a profession that is honourable and blameless.

Mental discipline/meditation (samādhi)

- Right Effort: The energetic will to develop a positive state of mind, free of craving and hatred. Fostering and nurturing wholesome states of mind. Preventing evil and unwholesome states of mind from arising, and ridding the self of existing ones.

- Right Mindfulness: Developing mindful awareness of the activities of the body; sensations and feelings; the activities of the mind; and ideas and concepts that affect one's understanding of reality – in particular how all of these arise and then disappear.

- Right Concentration: Working toward the state of mental focus necessary for effective meditation. This includes withdrawing the mind from automatic responses to sensations, eventually building up to developing a state of perfect, blissful awareness.

Wisdom (paññā)

- Right View: Understanding the Four Noble Truths and their explanation of reality – of how things really are. Right view is more than simply an intellectual grasp of the Four Noble Truths. It is to deeply understand them and to see the true nature of life.

- Right Intention: Committing to developing the necessary attitudes for learning from the Dharma. These include embodying the noble qualities of true wisdom, in particular: thoughts of love, non-violence, and selfless detachment or surrender.

These eight elements of the Noble Eightfold Path provide Buddhists with direction for attaining liberation in the form of realizing nirvāṇa. These are the Buddha's instructions for ending the suffering of individuals and for realizing complete freedom, peace and happiness. Also referred to as the "Middle Way", this path is designed to be practical and universally applicable, without going to extremes. For committed Buddhists, it is a rulebook for life.

THERE IS NO FEAR FOR ONE WHOSE MIND IS NOT FILLED WITH DESIRES.

GAUTAMA BUDDHA

SAṂSĀRA (REBIRTH)

In the Pāli and Sanskrit languages, the word saṃsāra means "world". It refers to the concept of repeated birth (or rebirth): that is, the idea that all life is cyclical. According to the concept of saṃsāra, all beings go through an endless cycle whereby they are born, have a mundane existence, and then die, only to be born again and repeat the cycle with another life.

The concept of saṃsāra has its origins in ancient India. First appearing in early Hindu texts, it is a philosophy that has a place in many Indian religions, including Hinduism, Jainism and Sikhism, as well as in Buddhism – although with slight differences in interpretation between religious groups.

In Buddhism, it is understood that the cycle of rebirth is uncomfortable, unsatisfying and laden with suffering. Buddhists believe that only by realizing nirvāṇa can one liberate themselves from saṃsāra and its related suffering. Attaining this liberation is both the founding goal and the most important purpose of Buddhism.

According to the Buddhist tradition, the driver of saṃsāra is karma. If saṃsāra were a vehicle, karma would be the fuel that keeps it going. It is also an individual's karma that is understood to determine where they are reborn. Wholesome karma can lead to a favourable rebirth, or even to moving a step closer to enlightenment.

Buddhists believe that there are six realms into which an individual can be reborn. It is said that one can be reborn as a human, an animal, a heavenly being, a hell being, a demi-god or a hungry ghost. A "hungry ghost" is a wretched being with a huge empty stomach yet no ability to eat. Apparently, being born into the realm of the hungry ghosts is caused by unwholesome karma: from having been greedy, envious and jealous, or from addictive or obsessive behaviour in a past life. In some Buddhist traditions, food offerings are left on altars for the hungry ghosts.

Although the goal of Buddhism is to realize nirvāṇa and to liberate oneself from saṃsāra, bodhisattvas (in the Mahāyāna tradition) voluntarily stay in saṃsāra – continuing to be reborn, in order to help others.

KARMA

Karma is a Sanskrit word meaning "deed" or "action". Karma, as introduced on page 10, is a foundational teaching in all schools of Buddhism. It also features in other Indian religions, including Sikhism, Hinduism and Jainism.

The term karma is often understood in the West to mean that, in life, every cause has an effect. Yet the Buddhist interpretation goes much deeper.

Buddhists believe that it is a being's karma that keeps them trapped in saṃsāra. Karma is the thread that connects an individual's past, present and future lives. A person carries their karma with them from lifetime to lifetime, and it is one's karma that determines which realm one will be reborn into next.

This may sound scary, but karma also contributes to liberation from saṃsāra, through the attainment of enlightenment. Have you ever played a board game in which you moved several tiles toward the finish line, only for something to happen that meant you had to move backward again? In a similar way, actions that generate wholesome karma move an individual closer to realizing nirvāṇa whereas actions that generate unwholesome karma are like backward steps.

It is also important to clarify how Buddhists define wholesome and unwholesome karma. The Buddha taught that there are three types of karma: that generated by the body (actions); that generated by speech (words); and that generated by the mind (thoughts). Crucially, karma is only believed to be created by "intentional" actions. For example, to intentionally kill another living being would generate unwholesome karma, but to accidentally stand on and kill an ant would have no karmic effect. Unintentional actions such as these are described as "neutral" or "ineffective". Sleeping, breathing and eating are also neutral actions, with no karmic impact.

When talking about karma, Buddhists do not use the terms good, bad or evil. Instead, they refer to wholesome, skilful and intelligent actions in relation to one's spiritual progress, such as acting with kindness, generosity, mindfulness or wisdom. The opposites of these are unskilful or unwholesome actions, such as acting from a place of hatred, greed or delusion.

How karma works

According to Buddhist teachings, all "intentional" actions produce results that the actor will eventually feel – a karmic result. Each intentional deed produces one of four karmic results: positive; negative; both some positive and some negative; or neither positive nor negative. The last of these is described as "karma without outflows" and is the type of karma produced by enlightened beings such as the Buddha, for whom the cycle of rebirth has already ended.

Buddhists' focus on karma has three purposes:

- ❧ To produce more wholesome karma, in order to move closer to realizing nirvāṇa and eventually become liberated from saṃsāra.

- ❧ To stop producing (or to produce less) unwholesome karma – as this moves one further away from realizing nirvāṇa.

- ❧ To ultimately stop producing any karma and feeding the cycle of rebirth, by realizing nirvāṇa. Thereafter, generating only "karma without outflows".

These goals provide good motivation for Buddhists to engage in wholesome and skilful actions. That said, the intention behind a deed is incredibly important. A skilful action that has a selfish motivation may not have favourable karmic results. To generate wholesome karma, the intention of an act should be pure: for example, to reduce the suffering of others.

Equally, a skilful action cannot "cancel out" an unskilful action. If an individual has generated unwholesome karma, such as by killing someone, donating lots of money to charity will not "even the score". To return to the board game analogy, this philanthropic act could move the individual a step forward on their spiritual journey – but only if the intention behind the donation was pure.

In Buddhist terms, every intentional act has a karmic impact, and this energy remains in the universe forever. It cannot be undone. The result may be experienced quickly (within this lifetime) or slowly, but it always affects rebirth.

Rebirth aside, the concept of karma offers all beings an opportunity to bring joy to others. Ultimately, it is about being conscious of the ripple effects generated by our actions.

ENLIGHTENMENT

What exactly is enlightenment? Despite its significance in the religion, enlightenment is one of the most difficult Buddhist concepts to explain. In fact, enlightened teachers often argue that it cannot be explained, only directly experienced.

Attaining enlightenment is said to happen slowly at first – and then quickly. Through consistent and concentrated meditation practice, the meditator gradually develops small moments of insight and understanding. These build up over time, until suddenly all the pieces of the puzzle are assembled and enlightenment comes in a flash.

In Buddhism, the lotus flower is often presented as a metaphor for enlightenment. Indeed, pictures and statues of the Buddha often show him sat atop a lotus flower. A lotus spends much of its life growing underwater, where it is dark and murky. This is said to represent the conditions of an unenlightened mind. Yet through consistent effort, the flower finally reaches the water's surface and breaks through, blossoming into a previously unseen world – bright and beautiful. This represents enlightenment.

Enlightenment relates to the teachings of anatman ("no self"), in Theravāda, and śūnyatā ("emptiness"), in Mahāyāna. These propose that there is no such thing as "you" and that the self is a mental illusion created by the ego. Rather, one's existence is said to be the result of causes and conditions – and that existence will cease when they do.

The illusion of being a permanent, independent and separate self is attractive. Yet clinging to this idea is, to Buddhists, the root of suffering – for it creates ideas of "us" and "them". This leads to fear, hate, jealousy and the concept of inferiority. Only when an individual abandons this illusion and sees the interconnectedness of all life can enlightenment occur.

Although we sometimes talk about "reaching" enlightenment, Buddhists do not actually consider enlightenment a destination. It is instead the moment when an individual finally rids themselves of the "dust in their eyes", as the Buddha put it, and sees the truth that was always present. Like a mountain in the fog, the truth of life is said to be always here. Yet it remains unseen until the fog of ignorance has cleared.

WHATEVER
PRECIOUS JEWEL
THERE IS IN
THE HEAVENLY
WORLDS, THERE
IS NOTHING
COMPARABLE
TO ONE WHO
IS AWAKENED.

GAUTAMA BUDDHA

Enlightenment and awakening: what's the difference?

In Buddhism, the terms "enlightenment" and "awakening" are generally treated as interchangeable and understood to mean the same thing. This can be confusing.

Some argue that awakening is a temporary moment of realization, whereas enlightenment is a permanent and comprehensive change in consciousness. Others use "awakened" to describe someone spiritually mature and on the path to attaining enlightenment. It could be said that when the Buddha saw the Four Sights, he became awakened. He "woke up" to the suffering in the world and the need to end it, which was the start of a spiritual journey that ultimately led to him realizing nirvāṇa.

Thus awakening could be described as a shift in perception: when someone becomes aware of their own ignorance and the helpless state of suffering they are living in, and then becomes determined to escape it, normally by practising the Dharma. From this perspective, it could be argued that awakening is the beginning point of an individual's spiritual journey, while enlightenment is the end.

NIRVĀṆA

Like awakening, "nirvāṇa" is another Buddhist term often used interchangeably with enlightenment. So, what's the difference? While exact interpretations vary, put simply, nirvāṇa can be considered a state of being, whereas enlightenment is more like a level of awareness.

Enlightenment refers to the level of awareness reached when an individual sheds the last of – to return to the Buddha's analogy – the "dust from their eyes". By contrast, nirvāṇa is thought to be the state of bliss that an individual dwells in once they can see the truth of life clearly at last.

By entering into the state of nirvāṇa, one may finally escape saṃsāra and become released from the effects of karma. Nirvāṇa is described as a transcendent state in which there is no suffering, no desire, no attachment and no sense of self.

Yet nirvāṇa should not be confused with something like "heaven". It is not believed to be a place at all, nor is it reached after death. Rather, nirvāṇa is supposedly the true nature of all sentient beings – it is just that dukkha prevents us from realizing this.

Consider a lake, which in its natural state is calm, peaceful and clear. Yet conditions such as wind cause waves on the water. Buddhists believe that, in a similar way, dukkha disrupts an individual's true, peaceful nature – and that only through learning to still the waters of our minds can we settle into the state of nirvāṇa that already exists within us. The proposed way to realize this true state is to follow the Noble Eightfold Path until one attains enlightenment.

There are some variations between the Theravāda and Mahāyāna understandings of nirvāṇa. For starters, Theravādins use the Pāli term "nibbāna". "Arhat" is the name Theravādins use for an enlightened being who has realized nibbāna "with remainders": that is, they have escaped their ignorance, cravings and aversions, yet remain conscious of them – thus, an arhat will only enter "complete nirvāṇa" upon death. This is known as "parinirvāṇa" or "parinibbāna". In Mahāyāna, bodhisattvas are said to voluntarily postpone parinirvāṇa and continue in the cycle of rebirth until such time that all beings realize nirvāṇa.

THE THREE POISONS (OR FIRES)

One common translation of the term "nirvāṇa" is "to blow out" or "to extinguish". This refers to what are known in Buddhism as the "Three Fires" that cause dukkha (or, more commonly, the "Three Poisons", because they are said to make a person sick). These are:

- Moha (ignorance/delusion)
- Rāga (greed/desire)
- Dveṣa (anger/hatred)

The Buddha taught that the five senses and consciousness of most people are constantly burning with these three fires. However, like all fires, greed, hatred and ignorance need fuel to continue burning. That fuel is said to be attachment. Thus, when one attains enlightenment and no longer has attachment, these fires have no more fuel and are "blown out". Once the fires are extinguished, what remains is nirvāṇa: one's true being – bliss.

Just as the Noble Eightfold Path teaches about "right views" and "right actions", the Three Fires/Poisons can be understood as "wrong views". These wrong views cause "wrong actions" (such as conflict, dishonesty or theft), which generate unwholesome karma, and, in turn, shackle one to saṃsāra.

Similarly, the Buddha is said to have explained the process of enlightenment using fire as a metaphor. When a fire is first extinguished, the embers remain warm, though less warm than before. In the same way, a freshly enlightened person may feel some residual heat from the Three Fires ("nirvāṇa with remainders"). Yet, over time, the embers settle into coolness (nirvāṇa). Likewise, it is said that blowing out the Three Fires can be frightening at first, but that the result (nirvāṇa) is calm and refreshing.

Buddhists understand the Three Fires, or Poisons, through the symbolism of animals. The pig represents ignorance and symbolizes the delusion that one can achieve lasting happiness (when, in fact, everything is impermanent and constantly changing). This leads to the rooster, which represents greed and attachment: the belief that money, a person or power will allow one to achieve lasting happiness. When unsatisfaction remains, this leads to anger/hatred, which is represented by a snake. The way to escape this process, Buddhists believe, is to pursue enlightenment by following the Noble Eightfold Path.

BUDDHAS

Did you know that the man we refer to as the Buddha is not the only buddha who has ever lived? There are said to have been anywhere between six and one thousand buddhas who came before Gautama Buddha – and new buddhas are expected in the future.

Before proceeding, let us clarify what we mean (and don't mean) by the term "buddha". A buddha is not a god or "divine creator", for there is no such thing in Buddhism. The term "buddha" most directly translates as "awakened one". So, how does a buddha differ from an arhat, or from a bodhisattva?

According to the Theravāda tradition, an arhat is a being who has achieved enlightenment under a teacher's guidance (such as by following the teachings of Gautama Buddha) and has realized nirvāṇa (with remainders). By contrast, one who attains enlightenment and realizes nirvāṇa on their own (as Gautama did) is called a "buddha". An enlightened bodhisattva has developed the wisdom of an enlightened being, but has vowed not to realize nirvāṇa and escape saṃsāra until all beings can join them.

The man we call the Buddha is also known as Shakyamuni Buddha ("Sage of the Shakya Clan") or else as "the buddha of our era". Shakyamuni Buddha reputedly taught that he would be followed, approximately 4,000 years later, by a new buddha, known as Maitreya. All Buddhist schools recognize this future buddha, although there is doubt over the sermon's authenticity.

Mahāyāna Buddhists also revere various buddhas who do not appear in the early scriptures and are thus not recognized by Theravāda Buddhism. These buddhas are understood to dwell in other realms and are sometimes called "celestial buddhas". Of note is Amitābha Buddha, the principal buddha of Pure Land Buddhism.

Vajrayāna Buddhism in turn recognizes buddhas who are unique to that school. These include several female buddhas – most notably Tārā, acknowledged as a buddha in Vajrayāna Buddhism and as a bodhisattva in other Mahāyāna traditions. Tārā is considered "the mother of liberation". Her name means "star" in Sanskrit and she is said to guide followers, like a star, on their spiritual path.

CHAPTER FOUR:
PRACTISING BUDDHISM

In this final chapter, we will explore some of the most common Buddhist practices, as well as their significance for those who live by them. Some practices you may already be familiar with. This is because many of the New Age and alternative spiritualities that we see in the modern world have been strongly influenced by the ancient traditions of Buddhism.

Do you already incorporate meditation or other mindfulness practices into your daily life? Or do you aspire to, and that is why you picked up this book? In either case, this chapter will have something to teach you.

It is important to note that while there are many ideas that one can take from Buddhism, to become a Buddhist is a lifelong commitment that requires dedicated and lengthy study. This is generally best undertaken with the assistance of a Buddhist community (such as a local group or temple) with whom one can learn and discuss the scriptures, involve oneself in Buddhist rituals and find support. We will explore some of these practices and rituals in the pages ahead.

MEDITATION

Buddhist meditation was once only undertaken by monks and nuns. Today, however, it is practised by laypeople too – and, indeed, by non-Buddhists as well. In Theravāda, meditation is known by the Pāli term "bhāvanā" ("to cultivate"). It is also referred to as "jhāna" (in Pāli) or as "dhyāna" (in Sanskrit), which is a form of mental training to clear the mind.

Meditation is normally undertaken in a seated position – commonly on the floor – and a popular pose is to sit cross-legged in what is known as the lotus position. (For a reminder of the significance of this name, see page 84.) The meditator should maintain a straight spine, settle the hands and minimize body movement during the practice. The eyes are normally closed, although some schools recommend adopting a soft gaze. The meditator then brings their awareness to their breath, quietly observing each inhale and exhale. They seek to maintain focus on this anchor in order to encourage other mental activity to quieten. Some meditators focus on other elements, but the breath is the most common anchor, as it is always with us – making meditation accessible anytime, anywhere.

Meditation practice can be undertaken alone, or in company. One can attend a meditation class or practise in a meditation hall (such as at a monastery). A meditation session can last from a few minutes to several hours. Yet regardless of the length, the purpose of meditation is always the same.

The purpose is to separate oneself from thoughts and feelings by calming the mind's activity, developing concentration and expanding awareness. Through this, the meditator can begin to see the world more clearly and experience the interconnectedness of all things. Meditation aims to open the heart and to foster emotional balance – this can lead the meditator to experience inner peace.

The goal of meditation is not to disappear into another realm, but simply to be in the present moment with complete awareness and without judgement. For Buddhists, another important objective is to avoid what is known as "duality". Thus the Buddhist approach to meditation considers the body and the mind as a single, united entity.

PEOPLE SACRIFICE THE PRESENT FOR THE FUTURE. BUT LIFE IS AVAILABLE ONLY IN THE PRESENT.

THÍCH NHẤT HẠNH

Buddhist meditation practices

All Buddhist meditation techniques are based on the insights into the nature of existence that the Buddha developed on his spiritual journey – as well as the guidelines that he subsequently established for living a constructive and wholesome life. It is from these that all Buddhist meditation methods have arisen.

Although different branches of Buddhism place varying emphasis on the importance of meditation, all schools consider it an essential component of the path to enlightenment. That said, for Buddhists, meditation is not just a means to an end, but rather a way of life.

There are numerous Buddhist meditation methods and each has a unique purpose. For example, a practice may be concentrative, generative, reflective, receptive or – most commonly – a combination of all the above, but with a particular stress on one aspect.

Let us now explore some of the most popular techniques. It must be noted that this is an overview rather than an exhaustive list. It may, however, assist you in choosing which type of meditation you would like to explore in the future.

Samatha ("mind-calmness" meditation)

As mentioned on page 17, Samatha is a form of concentrative meditation designed to calm and focus the mind through paying attention to the natural rhythm of the breath. As thoughts enter the mind, the meditator is invited to observe them without judgement or reaction, and to then let them go.

This type of meditation can include counting the breath on each inhale and exhale (up to ten), as a way to develop concentration and reduce distraction. Alternatively, the meditator may focus their visual and mental attention on an external object in front of them, such as a photo of the Buddha or the centre of a flower.

With commitment, regular Samatha meditation is said to cultivate great inner peace, clarity and happiness. However, its main purpose is to develop the necessary concentration skills to foster insight into the true nature of life, as this is the path to enlightenment. Samatha meditation is the perfect complement to and preparation for Vipassanā meditation, which we will explore next.

Vipassanā ("insight" meditation)

As mentioned in Chapter One, Vipassanā meditation is the central meditation practice of Theravāda Buddhists. It is practised by other Buddhist schools as well, but with adaptations.

The basic practice involves focusing the attention on the arising and passing away of physical sensations in each of the different parts of the body. Crucially, the meditator is encouraged to observe objectively, without reaction or judgement, regardless of whether the sensation is pleasant or unpleasant. Instead, they are to observe how each sensation is impermanent, ever-fluctuating and dissipates without their control.

The Vipassanā technique works with an individual's innate curiosity to develop their wisdom about the true nature of their experiences. It helps the meditator to view their own mind with clarity and to experience freedom from dissatisfaction.

Vipassanā is one of the most accessible forms of meditation to learn, thanks to a network of centres around the world offering free/by donation courses to people of all faiths. These are typically ten-day, silent, residential retreats that are designed to give a thorough introduction to the technique.

Metta ("loving-kindness" meditation)

Metta is a generative meditation aimed at increasing one's feelings of love and kindness toward all sentient beings. This is achieved using a combination of imagination, memory and awareness of bodily sensations – making it a good method to practise after learning the Vipassanā technique.

The meditator begins by generating feelings of loving-kindness (Metta), perhaps by recalling a recent act of kindness received, and by observing the physical sensations that the memory triggers. Alternatively, they may imagine a golden light spreading throughout their body.

Generally, the practice begins by meditating on objects for which it is easiest to arouse Metta, such as directing kind wishes to oneself. The meditator then moves progressively outward, perhaps next radiating love to a beloved person or pet, before eventually extending loving-kindness to more difficult parties, such as enemies.

Metta meditation is said to be an effective way to eliminate feelings of hatred or anger generated by the ego. Through Metta, boundaries like "friend" or "enemy" fade away, leaving only a pure flow of love – extending to all beings everywhere.

Zazen ("sitting Zen" meditation)

Zazen is a kind of receptive meditation. It is based on a belief in the significance of being in the present moment for connecting to the true nature of reality.

Zazen is the main meditation of Zen Buddhists and the most important part of their Buddhist practice. Consequently, Zen Buddhist monks typically spend eight to ten hours a day in meditation.

Zazen meditation generally involves sitting calmly in the lotus position, with the eyes open, and being fully receptive to whatever experiences arise, without passing judgement on them. The meditator avoids fantasizing about or desiring to change things. If they notice their mind wandering, they bring their attention back to the anchor of the breath. In some schools of Zen, meditators perform Zazen facing a wall. In others, meditators sit in a circle, facing one another.

A very similar Zen practice is Shikantza or "just sitting". In this, the meditator lets go of all activities – even focusing on the breath – giving the mind nothing to do. Even the intention to attain enlightenment should be dropped. The idea is to avoid activating the "self" and to become at one with nothingness.

Deity yoga ("visualization" meditation)

Deity yoga is the central form of meditation practised by the Tibetan and Vajrayāna schools of Buddhism. It is a reflective meditation.

Although there are some exceptions, most Buddhists do not consider deities to be gods (in the traditional sense) or supernatural beings. Rather, they are enlightened beings – regarded as archetypes or symbols of an awakened one – that the meditator can use to tap into the buddha qualities that lie dormant within themselves.

One approach to deity yoga is to visualize a particular deity (it could be the Buddha, a form of Tara, or any other Buddhist deity). The meditator then focuses on the qualities of that deity, which may help them to understand what traits they want to emulate and how they could move closer to attaining enlightenment.

Said to be even more transformative is when the meditator imagines themselves "as" a particular deity, in their form and reciting their mantras. Imagining oneself as the end result – already enlightened – is said to help such qualities to germinate and come to fruition more swiftly.

Walking meditation ("meditation in motion")

Walking meditation is practised by many Buddhist traditions and is a core practice in the schools of Theravāda and Zen (which calls it "kinhin"). It is designed to complement seated meditation and to maintain concentration between sessions. It is also, however, an important practice in its own right.

There is some variation in how different schools practise this meditation, but essentially it involves paying close attention to the process of walking, maintaining awareness throughout. It is about learning to remain present and mindful, even while in motion.

As well as paying attention to the breath, the meditator is encouraged to observe the sensations in their legs and feet as they come into contact with the ground, the contraction of muscles and other bodily sensations. The meditator generally moves slowly and may purposefully stop and start, in order to stay alert to changes in sensation. Walking meditation may be done alone, or walking in single file with a group.

Practised regularly, walking meditation is said to improve concentration, reduce anxiety and depression, improve overall health (including digestion and the immune system) and foster a deeper connection to nature.

Chanting ("meditating with the voice")

Chanting is sometimes described as "sound meditation" or "meditating with the voice". All Buddhist traditions involve chanting to some extent. In particular, it is the central devotional practice of Pure Land and Nichiren Buddhists.

Put simply, chanting involves speaking or singing a word or phrase over and over again. Buddhists use chanting both as a way of learning and of showing devotion to the teachings of the Buddha, which often form the contents of Buddhist chants. Chants may also include mantras, requests for protection or reminders of vows and ethics. They may be sung in Pāli, Sanskrit or in a language local to where they are being practised.

Understanding the words of a chant (or indeed, being a good singer) is not essential in order to benefit from this technique. Rather, it is the repetitive cycle of the chants that is thought to generate a meditative energy – suspending conceptual thinking and providing a different level of access to the ancient wisdom of the Dharma. Collective chanting is said to have further positive effects, including generating a sense of community among the Sangha.

Mantra ("sacred utterances")

A mantra is a sacred word or phrase used by Buddhists to support their meditation practice. The reciting of mantras is an ancient Indian tradition, far older than Buddhism. Today, however, it forms a part of all Buddhist schools – especially Vajrayāna – albeit with adaptations.

Mantras may be chanted, spoken or repeated silently in the mind. Their use is said to focus the mind and to transform it to a higher state. For Theravādins, the principal function of using a mantra is to nurture concentration in meditation. However, in the Mahāyāna tradition the use of mantras has a higher purpose: to request the protection of buddhas and bodhisattvas, or to invoke enlightened qualities within oneself.

The most commonly used, sacred and powerful of all the Buddhist mantras is "Om Mani Padme Hum". Although beyond direct translation, this mantra is understood to acknowledge the divine self that Buddhists believe we all have within us. Tibetan Buddhists use this mantra to call on Avalokiteśvara – the bodhisattva of compassion – and believe that its chanting can help them to embody compassion within themselves.

Meditation in the West

Over time, Buddhist meditation practices have spread far beyond the lands of their origins. Meditation is no longer solely the preserve of Buddhists, nor used only as a tool for spiritual enlightenment. In fact, you may have been practising a Buddhist technique of meditation without even realizing it!

This spread has been rapid in the last half century, during which meditation has gained popularity in the West. More recently, this has been accelerated by the rise of technology – including the development of a range of meditation apps, available on smartphones and tablets.

Similarly, Western audiences have a growing appetite for New Age and alternative spiritualities and therapies – hatha yoga, t'ai chi and meditation among them. Often, these are pursued in order to support physical or mental health goals, rather than as spiritual activities. Indeed, meditation is now recognized as an effective therapy for improving the management of stress, pain and depression, and for boosting the immune system. Today, there is much scientific evidence supporting meditation's benefits to health and happiness – backing up what age-old practitioners of meditation have always known.

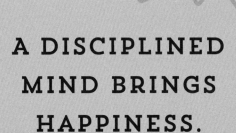

A DISCIPLINED MIND BRINGS HAPPINESS.

GAUTAMA BUDDHA

MINDFULNESS AND CLEAR COMPREHENSION

In the West, one often hears the terms "meditation" and "mindfulness" used interchangeably, but they are not the same thing. However, they are similar and, in many ways, intertwined. So, what's the difference?

Meditation is normally regarded as a formal, seated practice, during which a meditator spends a specific, focused amount of time tuned inward. By contrast, one can practise mindfulness anywhere, at any time, with anyone, throughout the day.

Mindfulness is the act of simply being present in whatever one is doing: of paying attention, rather than allowing the mind to wander to other thoughts, desires or worries. Many of us will be familiar with a "runaway mind", yet according to a Harvard study, a wandering mind causes unhappiness. Mindfulness is an opportunity to become actively mindful of not only the world around us, but of our movements, thoughts, actions – and of the impacts of our actions on those close to us.

In Buddhism, mindfulness is a foundational practice and is seen as key for living an ethically wholesome life. Mindfulness is considered a wise and intentional act, indivisible from following the steps of the Noble Eightfold Path.

In Theravāda, mindfulness is known by the Pāli term "sati", meaning "memory". Thus, mindfulness is "remembering" to stay in the present moment – as opposed to "forgetting" and letting the mind wander. Practising mindfulness during one's meditation practice is said to help strengthen this muscle for the rest of the day, but the practice is not synonymous with meditation itself.

For Buddhists, a key benefit of mindfulness is the cultivation of clear comprehension or consciousness, which is an important step toward attaining enlightenment. Clear comprehension is a sharpness of mind that enables one to detect one's own thoughts and intentions in daily life before these become processed into speech or actions: for example, having the wisdom of attention to notice feelings of ill will and switch them to good intentions before opening one's mouth to speak. This ensures Right Speech and Right Action, as recommended by the Noble Eightfold Path.

BUDDHIST MONKS AND MONASTICISM

Buddhism has one of the oldest traditions of organized monkhood (or "monasticism") in the world. Buddhist monks ("bhikkhu") and nuns ("bhikkunis") are individuals who give up their ordinary pursuits and material possessions to dedicate part or all of their lives to spiritual goals – much like the wandering ascetics who were the Buddha's first disciples.

Today, Buddhist monastics often live in monasteries, separated by gender, as all monastics take a vow of chastity. Monks and nuns follow the Vinaya: a strict code of conduct, believed to have been largely established by the Buddha himself. Three variations of the Vinaya exist today, governing monastic life in different regional traditions, and nuns must observe eight additional rules to those followed by monks.

Buddhist monastics are responsible for preserving and spreading the Buddha's teachings, as well as for guiding Buddhist laypeople in their practice. This includes providing a living example of Buddhist discipline by observing a minimalist life of good moral character, focused on studying the Dharma and practising meditation. Monastics also serve as a "field of merit" for laypeople, who may accumulate merit by providing them with food and other essentials.

There are many reasons why Buddhists choose a life of monasticism. For some, it is an opportunity to immerse themselves in the Dharma and to spend uninterrupted hours in meditation and study. It is also a chance to serve one's community and to help others, as well as to contribute to the preservation of the Dharma for future generations. In some traditions, it is believed that becoming a monastic accumulates merit for both oneself and one's family. Meanwhile, in disadvantaged areas, some people (especially children) join the monastic community in order to gain access to food, education and housing.

While exact monastic traditions vary between countries and schools, all promote a life of austerity. Most monastics maintain few possessions and are predominantly (if not solely) reliant on donations to cover their daily needs. They typically rise at around four o'clock in the morning and they might only eat one meal per day. Monastics also generally maintain shaved heads and wear plain, matching robes.

Buddhist monasticism is not an easy life – and is certainly not for everyone. However, many monks and nuns find the monastic lifestyle one of peace, happiness and liberation.

REFUGE

An important religious practice in Buddhism is the act of "taking refuge". New Buddhists who wish to make their commitment to their faith "official" take refuge as a form of initiation ceremony. It is a ritual that has been undertaken since Buddhism's early days.

Buddhists take refuge in what are known as the "Three Jewels" or the "Triple Gem". These are: the Buddha (teacher), the Dharma (teachings) and the Sangha (community) – three precious resources that form the core of all Buddhists' faith.

There are some variations between the Theravāda, Mahāyāna and Vajrayāna traditions, but broadly, when a new Buddhist commits to take Triple Gem refuge, they:

- Accept the Buddha as their enlightened teacher and role model.
- Accept the Dharma as the path to freedom from suffering and commit to its study.
- Take refuge in the worldwide community of lay and monastic Buddhists that form the Sangha, in the understanding that this "family" will support them on their spiritual journey.

It is important to note that the act of taking refuge is not about showing devotion to Buddhism, but rather about making a commitment to oneself to escape suffering. It is about acknowledging one's inner buddha-nature, and the Triple Gem as the path to uncover it. As such, it is not the act of taking refuge that benefits a person's life, but following that up with dedicated study and practice of the Dharma – with the goal of eventually realizing nirvāṇa.

Buddhists who have taken refuge do their best to live according to the main advice of the teachings, including participating in meaningful activities, working on taming their minds, and not harming others. They renew their commitment to the Triple Gem regularly, to reinforce their focus and dedication. Indeed, many Buddhists repeat the refuge prayer at the beginning of each day, gathering or practice session.

Taking refuge is ultimately a personal commitment and thus can be undertaken at any time, anywhere, by anyone. However, official refuge ceremonies are normally overseen by a Buddhist monastic, often in a temple.

RESTRAINT AND RENUNCIATION

The Buddha taught that unhappiness is caused by one's cravings and attachments. Hence, when one renounces (or lets go of) such cravings, one becomes free.

For Buddhists, renunciation is about letting go of anything that binds them to ignorance and suffering. This could include attachment to certain beliefs and opinions, people and material possessions, and to unhealthy habits and behaviours.

Lay Buddhists let go of material possessions through acts of giving. Buddhist monks and nuns go a step further, however; upon entering monastic life, normally give up all non-essential possessions – as well as their hair, the use of money, a varied wardrobe and eating after noon. Buddhist monastics are also expected to renounce all unwholesome actions and desires, and to practise celibacy.

It is believed that renunciation assists a monastic's inner transformation. Through renunciation they may discover that what they had assumed to be necessary for happiness may not have been its cause at all. Renunciation is considered an opportunity to liberate themselves from lust and to experience freedom from compulsion.

The Buddha is said to have taught "Anupassanā": a technique that includes contemplating the negative consequences of sensual pleasure. Additionally, he taught "Indriyasaṃvara": restraint of the senses prior to meditation.

The Buddha also encouraged restraint toward food, encouraging followers to eat in moderation rather than greedily. Monastics therefore do not usually eat after noon. Some Buddhists also undertake periods of fasting.

Restraint and renunciation form part of the Right Intention aspect of the Noble Eightfold Path. Buddhists come to see greediness as simply a temporary distraction from suffering, which ultimately keeps one from realizing nirvāṇa.

For lay Buddhists, Right Intention means understanding the temporary nature of possessions and practising non-attachment, restraint and generosity. Lay Buddhists may also attend meditation retreats, where (for a limited time) they renounce speech, sexual activity, reading, writing, entertainment and, by following a strict schedule, control over their food and how they spend their time. This is not an easy experience, but it is believed to create the ideal environment for spiritual practice.

VEGETARIANISM AND ANIMAL ETHICS

Many people assume that all Buddhists are required to be vegetarians. Yet the truth is more complex.

The Buddha provided guidelines for moral behaviour (the Five Precepts), which Buddhists follow like vows. The first of these directs them to neither kill nor intentionally cause harm to any living being. Buddhists are instead instructed to extend equal respect, compassion and kindness to all sentient beings.

As conscious beings, animals are believed to have innate buddha-nature and to be capable of enlightenment, just like humans. To cause intentional harm or death to animals is said to generate unwholesome karma, which moves one further away from realizing nirvāṇa.

Despite this, the Buddha never explicitly promoted vegetarianism. Indeed, it is believed that he opposed vegetarianism being made compulsory for Buddhist followers. He did, however, forbid followers from killing animals for food, or to trade in meat – as stated in the "Right Livelihood" part of the Noble Eightfold Path. The Buddha also listed animals that should never be eaten, including elephant, horse, leopard and snake.

Yet if his monks were offered meat by a layperson, they were instructed to receive it gratefully and eat it – so long as the meat was leftovers and an animal had not been slaughtered especially to feed them.

In general, the Buddha encouraged his followers to take the "Middle Way" and not be too extreme in any of their pursuits, opinions or attachments. As such, Buddhists who are vegetarian are warned against becoming fanatically attached to this – as this attachment itself could cause suffering.

Today, most Mahāyāna schools encourage vegetarianism, often growing vegetables in their monasteries. Theravādins, however, see vegetarianism as a personal choice. Theravāda monastics generally rely on donations and thus eat whatever they are offered. Even the Dalai Lama (XIV) is known to have begun eating meat in recent years, for health reasons. Historically, Tibetan Buddhists have tended not to be vegetarian, as it is difficult to grow vegetables in Tibet.

In conclusion, there is no simple answer to the question of Buddhist vegetarianism. It remains a much-debated topic among Buddhists.

BUDDHIST TEMPLES AND RITUALS

Buddhists visit temples to worship, practise and study, and to connect with the Sangha. Temples may be independent buildings or form a part of a monastery.

In general, temples are designed to represent the pure and peaceful environment of a buddha. However, their architecture varies dramatically between regions. They are always made to the finest quality and designed to symbolize the five elements: earth, fire, air, water and wisdom. This is particularly evident in the architecture of pagodas: tiered towers with multiple eaves that are common in South and East Asia.

The most important part of any Buddhist temple is the shrine (and many Buddhists also have smaller shrines in their homes). Here one will find a (often very large) statue of the Buddha – if not several. In front of each statue is normally an altar, where Buddhists lay offerings of food, water, flowers, candles and incense. Buddhists remove their shoes before entering a shrine room, as a mark of respect, and bow to the statue before reciting the Three Jewels or Refuges.

At temples, Buddhists chant, meditate, make offerings and listen to sermons (or "Dharma talks") from senior Buddhist monastics. In parts of Asia, however, Buddhists also regularly visit stupas. These dome-shaped buildings are said to contain relics – such as a hair or tooth – of the Buddha himself or of an important disciple or teacher. Buddhists do not enter stupas, but instead mindfully walk around them in a clockwise direction while reciting mantras, meditating or praying.

This is a way for Buddhists to pay tribute, while also cultivating their minds and perhaps accumulating merit. The Buddha reportedly often mentioned "circumambulating" objects in his teachings, saying that this purified unwholesome karma and helped to ensure a favourable rebirth. Buddhists also circumambulate temples, statues, sacred mountains and even people. At least three rotations (to honour the Three Jewels) is customary.

Buddhists may also make pilgrimages to sacred sites, to both intensify their practice and to generate merit. The main Buddhist pilgrimage circuit takes in four significant sites: that of the Buddha's birth, nirvāṇa, first teaching and death. Buddhist pilgrims have travelled this route for millennia.

MERIT-MAKING

One might assume that meditation is the most-practised Buddhist activity. In fact, beyond the West, the primary practice of Buddhists around the world is the cultivation of merit.

Buddhists believe that merit is an intangible force generated by good deeds done. This links to generating wholesome karma, so as to ensure a favourable rebirth and move closer to enlightenment. Accumulating merit is also said to improve a person's mind, inner well-being and circumstances. Furthermore, there is a custom of sharing one's merit with a deceased loved one, to help them in their new existence.

The Pāli Canon states that merit may be earned in three ways (arranged in order of difficulty): Giving ("dāna-maya") to charity or to Buddhist monks and nuns, or other acts of generosity; Virtue ("sīla-maya") – upholding the Precepts and following the Noble Eightfold Path; and Mental Development ("bhāvāna-maya"), which encompasses meditation, reciting mantras, pilgrimage and studying the Dharma.

Merit-making activities are an essential part of Buddhists' daily rituals and festivals. According to Buddhist teachings, such activities are of benefit to both the individual and to the wider world.

MY RELIGION IS VERY SIMPLE. MY RELIGION IS KINDNESS.

THE DALAI LAMA (XIV)

CONCLUSION

So, there you have it! Whether you're planning on continuing your research into Buddhism or aspiring to incorporate Buddhist values into your life, this book will hopefully have provided all the information that you need to get started.

As we have learned, Buddhism is a religious philosophy with a rich history. It is a faith of considerable diversity – and that might be its greatest merit. It has the flexibility to be understood and adopted by people from all walks of life. Whoever you are, there is probably something in Buddhism that resonates with you – something that you can take forward in order to make your life a little happier. You don't have to adopt or agree with all of it. Take what speaks to you and leave the rest.

At its heart, Buddhism is about wisdom and compassion. It is about generating not only freedom from suffering, but also happiness for all living beings. So, to leave you with an instruction from the Buddha himself: go out there and "radiate boundless love toward the entire world".

FURTHER READING

If you've enjoyed this book and would like to read more about the topics covered, these websites and books are a great place to start:

Websites

Tricycle – Buddhism for Beginners
    www.tricycle.org/beginners
Alan Peto – Buddhism Explained for Westerners
    www.alanpeto.com

Books

Opening the Door of Your Heart, Ajahn Brahm (2010)
How to Meditate, Pema Chödrön (2021)
Buddhism for Beginners, Thubten Chodron (2001)
The Heart of the Buddha's Teaching, Thích Nhất Hạnh (1999)
Peace is Every Step, Thích Nhất Hạnh (1992)

THE LITTLE BOOK OF KARMA

Isabelle Loynes

Paperback
ISBN: 978-1-80007-683-9

One kind act can go a long way, and even the smallest deed can have a profound impact. Learn how to tap into the awesome power of karma with this little book, offering everything you need to know about this ancient source of spiritual wisdom. You'll soon find that just a few small acts of kindness and compassion can brighten your outlook and bring balance to your life. Because what goes around comes around.

THE LITTLE BOOK OF REIKI

Stephanie Drane

Paperback

ISBN: 978-1-80007-684-6

Reiki is a Japanese complementary therapy with the aim of bringing balance and well-being to the body, mind and spirit. Drawing on the energy of the universe, Reiki seeks to direct and apply this life force to restore health and harmony in the individual. From the history and etymology of Reiki to techniques and exercises to practise self-Reiki, this beginner's guide will help you to discover what Reiki is and how you can introduce it into your daily routine for a healthier, happier life.

Have you enjoyed this book? If so, find
us on Facebook at Summersdale Publishers,
on Twitter at @Summersdale and on Instagram
and Tiktok at @summersdalebooks and get
in touch. We'd love to hear from you!

www.summersdale.com